PENGUIN BOOKS

ZAFARNAMA

Navtej Sarna is a diplomat and author. Formerly the foreign office spokesman and India's ambassador to Israel, he is Secretary in India's foreign ministry.

He is the author of the novels *We Weren't Lovers Like That* and *The Exile* and the short story collection *Winter Evenings*. His non-fiction works include *The Book of Nanak* and *Indians at Herod's Gate*.

Zafarnama

Guru Gobind Singh

Translated and introduced by
Navtej Sarna

PENGUIN BOOKS
An imprint of Penguin Random House

PENGUIN BOOKS

USA | Canada | UK | Ireland | Australia
New Zealand | India | South Africa | China

Penguin Books is part of the Penguin Random House group of companies
whose addresses can be found at global.penguinrandomhouse.com

Published by Penguin Random House India Pvt. Ltd
4th Floor, Capital Tower 1, MG Road,
Gurugram 122 002, Haryana, India

Penguin
Random House
India

First published by Penguin Books India 2011
This paperback edition published 2015

This edition copyright © Penguin Books India 2011
Translation and introduction copyright © Navtej Sarna 2011

All rights reserved

10 9 8 7 6 5 4 3 2

ISBN 9780143425557

Typeset in Sabon by Eleven Arts, Delhi

Printed at Repro India Limited

www.penguin.co.in

MIX
Paper from
responsible sources
FSC® C047271

To my parents, Mohinder Singh and Surjit Sarna,
who bequeathed to me a passion for literature

CONTENTS

CONTENTS

TRANSLATOR'S NOTE

Translating an early eighteenth-century text of Persian verse into present-day English would always have been a challenge. At least two sets of problems compounded the difficulties. First, the problems caused by the transcription of the text of the *Zafarnama* preserved in the *Dasam Granth* from Persian script into Gurmukhi. This transcription was often accompanied by the introduction of material changes by scribes, sometimes to reflect a particular historical viewpoint but equally often because of difficulties in interpreting the text or a desire to amend existing readings to ones that seemed to make more sense to the copyist. These Gurmukhi texts, already at variance with the original and with each other, in turn became a basis for further interpretation and commentary. Secondly, Indian Persian, which had diverged significantly by the late Mughal period from classical Persian, both in literary terms as well as in pronunciation, could only be reproduced imperfectly in the Gurmukhi script, thus adding another layer of variations. Therefore, I was confronted with several choices even before coming to the actual process of translation. Primarily, I had to decide which particular text to rely on. Then I had to choose how to depict the transliteration—in Indian Persian, or in Persian as it is spoken today, or in a generally accepted form which is as close to Indian Persian as the Gurmukhi script will allow. I decided in favour of the last option.

Existing translations and commentaries of the *Zafarnama*—in Punjabi or English—further multiplied these textual distortions through choices dictated again not only by the complexity of script and grammar but also by the historical gloss that each translator or commentator wanted to put on the text. There are very traditional interpretations and there are more modern, often conflicting, ones. In this attempt to put forth an authentic translation and, inevitably, an interpretation of the *Zafarnama*, I have been only too aware of these layers of potential confusion and can by no means say that I have overcome them all. Placing myself as a writer and translator and not as a scholar or historian, I have tried to balance the differing interpretations by the felicitous tool of footnotes, leaving the academic battles for better-qualified people.

Huge debts need to be acknowledged. For the Introduction, I have relied largely on Harbans Singh's *Guru Gobind Singh*, J.D. Cunningham's *A History of the Sikhs*, Khushwant Singh's *A History of the Sikhs* and Patwant Singh's *The Sikhs*. For the translation of the *Zafarnama*, I relied on the Gurmukhi text (and to a large extent, the interpretation) as translated by Bhai Vir Singh in his *Kalgidhar Chamatkar* and also consulted the more non-traditional translation by Christopher Shackle and Arvind-pal Singh Mandair in their *Teachings of the Sikh Gurus*. When lost, I would turn for guidance to the free translation of the *Zafarnama* into Punjabi by my father Mohinder Singh Sarna as part of his epic poem *Chamkaur*.

This work would not have been possible without the guidance of Dr Jeevan Deol. I am deeply indebted to him for helping me choose from amongst the multiple texts and interpretations and for immeasurably improving the rendering of the Persian as well as its translation. The scholarship and generosity was his; the mistakes that may still persist are solely mine.

And my thanks too to those who persistently prodded me to complete this work: Ravi Singh at Penguin India and Avina at home.

INTRODUCTION

Chun kar az hameh heelate dar guzasht
Halal ast burdan bi-shamsher dast

When all has been tried, yet
Justice is not in sight,
It is then right to pick up the sword,
It is then right to fight.

These are perhaps the most often quoted words of the *Zafarnama*, the 'Epistle of Victory', written by Guru Gobind Singh to Aurangzeb, the last of the great Mughal emperors of India, sometime in 1705. Besides the obvious tone of fearless defiance, they are emblematic of the poetic power and philosophical underpinning that is so evident in the *Zafarnama*, like in all the writings of the prolific tenth Guru of the Sikhs.

Written in Persian, its 111 stirring stanzas echoing the influence of Firdausi's *Shahnama*, the letter holds up an uncompromising mirror to the Mughal emperor. It indicts him and his commanders against a spiritual frame of judgement and exposes their lack of morality in governance as well as in the conduct of war. It foresees the end of an empire that is dominated by falsehood and whose innards have been hollowed out by spiritual decay. At the same time, it is a brilliant exposition of the Guru's own spiritual beliefs, his political and moral philosophy and the true nature of God and Creation.

An understanding of the *Zafarnama* presupposes some familiarity with the immediate historical events it refers to—the battles between the Sikhs and the Mughal army along with the supporting hill rajas, the evacuation of Anandpur by the Sikhs on the basis of false oaths sworn on the Quran by the Mughals, the historic battle of Chamkaur, the martyrdom of the Guru's four sons, and so on. To grasp the full philosophical message of the *Zafarnama* it is necessary to delve deeper and to trace, even if briefly, the emergence of the Sikh faith as an independent religion as well as its development as a political movement that ultimately challenged Mughal rule in northern India. In short, one has to go back to the time when Guru Nanak (1469–1539) began the moral and spiritual renaissance of a populace steeped in ignorance and superstition. This renaissance was to become, under the guidance of the tenth Guru two centuries later, a miraculous transformation of the human spirit that would see an oppressed people fight bigotry and religious persecution with scarcely imaginable courage.

When Nanak, the first Guru, was born in 1469 in Talwandi, the times were marked by religious bigotry, moral decay and political persecution. The ordinary people had retreated into orthodoxy, blind superstition and ritualism perpetuated by a self-serving priesthood. In his own words:

> The dark times are like a knife,
> The kings are butchers,
> Dharma has taken wings and flown,
> In the dark night of falsehood,
> The moon of truth
> Cannot be seen.
>
> —*Var Majh*

Hope for an urgently needed moral and spiritual regeneration lay in the trends started by the Sufi movement in Islam and the

Bhakti movement in Hinduism, both based on a passionately personal expression of love for the Divine. To these movements, Guru Nanak brought an understanding purely his own which would take the idea of an individual's personal experience and expand it to a widespread religion for the common man, indeed an integrated philosophy of life that would be based not on ascetic denial but on an affirmation of the reality of this world with the ultimate truth.

Guru Nanak's message was simple and he spread it through his prolific writings and extensive travels in all directions: God was one and supreme. He was the all-pervading Creator—fearless, timeless and self-existent—who could be realized only through His own grace. All men were equal; discrimination on the basis of caste or creed as well as the suppression of women was to be denounced. He advocated the righteous life of a householder against that of the ascetic. This world is a reflection of Divine purpose and man's duty is to improve the condition of his fellow beings through love and compassion, through right conduct. Practical virtue, rather than abstract piety, is the preferred way. Honest work, charity and the remembrance of the true God's name is the path to salvation. He denounced the oppression and tyranny of the ruling classes, protesting against the invasion of Hindustan by Babur who had 'charged with his wedding party of sin from Kabul'. He lamented the suffering inflicted on innocent citizens, particularly the womenfolk. His reaction was not just of an eyewitness but also of a philosophical sage, a visionary and a poet. The shortcomings of the age, the profligacy of rulers, the nature of the Divine Will and the suffering that mankind has to endure when the cosmic principles on which the world rests are ignored were all brought out in his compositions which are renowned for their spiritual depth and literary beauty. This protest could be regarded as the genesis of the clash of the Sikh faith with the Mughal Empire.

When Nanak settled down in Kartarpur on the banks of the Ravi after more than twenty years on the road, he gathered around him a congregation which was a precursor to the community that was to follow. Here he taught the way of true worship of God, the discipline of true reflection and meditation as well as the rejection of outward form and false status based on caste or wealth. Here started the practice of kirtan—the singing of praises of God. Here too were seen the beginnings of the institution of langar, or the communal kitchen. A new community, with its own tradition of companionship, its values and beliefs was thus born in Punjab. In the immediate context of the *Zafarnama*, the words of the British historian, Cunningham, are appropriate: 'It was reserved for Nanak to perceive the true principles of reform, and to lay those broad foundations which enabled his successor Gobind to fire the minds of his countrymen with a new nationality, and give practical effect to the doctrine that the lowest is equal with the highest, in race as in creed, in political rights as in religious hopes.'[1]

The next four successors of Guru Nanak were to consolidate the evolving faith in different ways by their contributions. The first successor, Guru Angad, who had been a firm Hindu devotee of the Devi before he came under Nanak's influence, was chosen by Nanak over his own sons because of his devoted service to the community at Kartarpur. He moved to Khadur, where he continued to build a disciplined community, and developed a local script into a distinctive form of writing for the community's scriptures—the Gurmukhi script. He collected Nanak's hymns and made copies for each centre of the community, adding his contribution of short verses.

The third Guru, Amar Das, moved his centre to Goindwal on the river Beas and assiduously consolidated the new faith. He made the langar an integral part of the Sikh church—even Emperor Akbar is said to have eaten from the communal kitchen when he visited the Guru. He wrote extensively himself (891 of his hymns are included in the Guru Granth Sahib, the holy text of the Sikhs) and even

---

[1] J.D. Cunningham, *A History of the Sikhs* (1849).

compiled the writings of his predecessors, also adding many hymns of well-known Bhaktas like Namdev and Kabir. The congregation increased considerably during his time and he organized twenty-two *manjis* or centres, appointing local agents or *masands* to organize worship, initiate new disciples and collect offerings. He made very significant social innovations that were to form an important aspect of a distinct Sikh cultural identity, including the prohibition of the practices of sati and purdah, as well as the propagation of widow remarriage and inter-caste marriages.

The Guru-ship moved on thereafter to Ram Das, his devoted disciple and son-in-law, who chose to build a town by an expanse of water between the Ravi and the Beas. This town would get the name of Ramdaspur, and later, Amritsar; the expanse of water would house the Harmandir Sahib (the Golden Temple). The Sikhs were encouraged to make contributions in cash, kind and service for the excavation of the tank and the growth of the town; in fact, the spirit of voluntary labour remains strong in Sikhism to this day. His compositions further enriched the growing body of religious literature and included the marriage hymns that are sung in Sikh weddings.

Introducing the principle of heredity (though not primogeniture), Guru Ram Das nominated his youngest son Arjan Mal as his successor, arousing the anger of his eldest, Prithi Chand. Dissension in issues of succession was not unknown in the development of the Sikh faith and, in fact, had been in play since the sons of Guru Nanak; it lay behind the need for each of the three successors of Nanak to move to or found a new town. Guru Arjan completed the Harmandir Sahib, asking Mian Mir, a Muslim Sufi saint, to lay the foundation stone. The simple and modest temple, as it then was, had none of the trappings of extravagance usually associated with such buildings. It was lower than the surrounding land and not towering above; it had four entrances and was thus open to people of all castes. The Harmandir was to undergo destruction and desecration many times at the hands of invaders such as Ahmad

Shah Abdali, and would be given its present spectacular form by Maharaja Ranjit Singh in the nineteenth century.

During Guru Arjan's time, Amritsar grew not merely as a place of pilgrimage but as a spiritual centre and source of inspiration for the Sikhs. To provide a core to this inspiration, Guru Arjan began work on compiling the Sikh scriptures with his maternal uncle Bhai Gurdas as his scribe. The compilation included the writings of the first four Gurus as well as his own; in addition, the writings of Muslim and Hindu saints like Farid, Namdev, Kabir, Ravi Das and many others who were of kindred spiritual belief were also included. The result was the Adi Granth, consisting then of more than 5,000 hymns, and classified according to thirty-one ragas according to which they would be sung. The Adi Granth would be given its final shape by Guru Gobind Singh.

On 16 August 1604, Guru Arjan installed the Adi Granth in the Harmandir with Bhai Buddha as the first Granthi or reader. During these years, which were marked by benevolent relations with Emperor Akbar, the Sikh community flourished with a sense of a distinct identity and was not restricted to Punjab alone. Sikhs could be found in Kashmir and Kabul, Delhi and Agra. This good fortune, however, came to an end with the death of Akbar. Emperor Jahangir was uncomfortable with the popularity of Guru Arjan and was keen to put an end to the 'false traffic' that he believed the house of the Guru had carried on for several generations. He was also under the impression that the Guru had supported the rebellious prince Khusrau against him. Encouraged by the Guru's detractors around him—both orthodox Muslims and orthodox Hindus—Jahangir ordered the arrest of the Guru and his family. In Lahore, the Guru was severely tortured and made to sit on a hot plate while sand was poured on him. Ultimately, the Guru achieved martyrdom when he drowned in the river Ravi. But before that he had sent word that his eleven-year-old son Hargobind should be nominated the sixth Guru of the Sikhs.

The pacific martyrdom of Guru Arjan was to start a new tradition in the faith—the demonstration of one's convictions through the ultimate sacrifice. It showed how one man, without the use of physical strength and force, could defeat oppression morally. In the words of the Sikh savant Dr Balbir Singh, Guru Arjan showed through his martyrdom that 'the oppressor can do no more than take your life, and even when he takes it does not fall in his hands and you do not lose it, because it was never yours to begin with; you had already handed it over to your Master.'[2]

But Guru Hargobind knew that his father's martyrdom would not awaken the comatose conscience of the oppressive regime. His answer was the introduction of a martial spirit into the pacific faith; the Sikhs were taught to take up arms, but only in self-defence and for the right cause. Wearing two swords around his waist—one for spirituality (*peeri*) and the other for temporal power (*meeri*)—he gathered a body of soldiers around him and spent much time on martial exercises and hunting. These developments were, in a way, a challenge to the state. The fledgling army clashed with the Mughals on several occasions and emerged victorious, showing that Mughal writ could be successfully challenged. A new spirit of armed defiance and pride in their prowess had entered the consciousness of the Sikhs which was celebrated by the singing of heroic ballads, accompanied by the blood-stirring strains of the sarangi at the Akal Takht, the new temporal seat of the faith built right across from the Harmandir Sahib which had already become the spiritual centre. There was a further accretion to a distinct identity with the Guru's renewal of the importance of Amritsar and his focus on strengthening community institutions. For the last decade of his life Hargobind retreated to the settlement of Kiratpur in the Siwalik hills on the banks of the Sutlej, choosing his grandson Har Rai to succeed him.

---

[2] Translated from Dr Balbir Singh's *Kalam di Karamat* (Bhai Veer Singh Sahitya Sadan, 1933).

Guru Har Rai was a man of peace and prayer, and his seventeen years as Guru were rather uneventful. For the most part he had to move deeper into the hills, yet he managed to travel extensively to spread Nanak's message. He did incur the wrath of Aurangzeb who saw him as siding with Dara Shikoh, his rival and brother, in the succession struggle. When the ruthless and despotic Aurangzeb succeeded to the Delhi throne after killing his brothers and imprisoning his father, he summoned Har Rai to Delhi. The Guru sent his son Ram Rai who succeeded in pleasing the emperor but only after deliberately misreading a verse from the Granth which the emperor had believed to be derogatory of Islam. This turned his father's mind away from Ram Rai and he appointed his second son, the five-year old Har Krishan, as his successor. The child-Guru was also summoned to Delhi by the emperor who wanted to pursue the issue of succession to his own advantage by supporting the claims of Ram Rai. However, Har Krishan was struck down by small pox, and before he died he indicated that an older person living in the village of Bakala would be the next Guru. This was none other than Tegh Bahadur—the youngest son of the sixth Guru, Hargobind—who had spent long years in meditation.

Troubled by envious kinsmen who resented his succession, Tegh Bahadur moved to a new centre that was to become one of the most revered places in Sikhism. This was the village of Makhowal in the Siwaliks. He renamed it Anandpur, the abode of bliss. Tegh Bahadur travelled extensively to far-flung congregations in the Gangetic plain—Delhi, Mathura, Agra, Allahabad, Varanasi. Then leaving his family in Patna, he went on further to Dhaka and Assam. It was at Patna that his only son, Gobind, was born on 22 December 1666.

Meanwhile Punjab was reeling under Mughal oppression. Aurangzeb had unleashed a frenzy of religious persecution, ordering the demolition of schools and temples of all infidels. The dreaded *jizya* tax was reimposed on all non-Muslims. Matters came to a head when a delegation of Kashmiri Pandits came to Guru Tegh Bahadur, requesting him to save them from the conversions being enforced by Aurangzeb's governor, Ifthikar Khan. After deliberating over the matter, the Guru stated that if the emperor could convert him to Islam, the Pandits would follow suit. This was a direct challenge to Aurangzeb who ordered that Tegh Bahadur be brought to Delhi in fetters. Tegh Bahadur did not wait for his captors but began moving towards Delhi of his own accord. When finally arrested, he was brought to Delhi in an iron cage on 5 November 1675.

The Mughals challenged the Guru to perform a miracle or convert to Islam. When he refused, three of his close companions who had joined him of their own volition were killed in his presence—one was sawn into two, the second boiled alive and the third burnt alive. Thereafter, the Guru himself was beheaded in the market square of Chandni Chowk; the revered Gurudwara Sisganj now stands at that spot. A terrible storm then raged through Delhi and during the storm, a humble Sikh called Jaita recovered the Guru's head and took it to Anandpur to the Guru's son Gobind. The body was similarly smuggled away by another follower—Lakhi Rai, a cotton merchant—to his own hut on Raisina hill and the hut was set afire to cremate the body. Gurudwara Rakabganj in Delhi is the solemn memorial in white marble built on this site.

Of his father's martyrdom, Guru Gobind Singh was to later write in *Bachitra Natak*:

> At the departure of Tegh Bahadur
> The world was shrouded in grief;
> Lamentations in the world of men,
> But in the world of God there was praise.

Guru Tegh Bahadur had demonstrated that the human soul could not be caged and that bravery was not only that of the sword. The truly courageous had no fear of death—death was not a punishment but a prize to which true warriors of the spirit had a right. It was not an end to be feared but a beginning of eternal life. A unique sacrifice had been made in defence of religious freedom; the spirit had notched up a great victory over despotism. The stage was set for a series of cataclysmic clashes. In the next round, steel would be infused in the soul by the sacrament of the double-edged dagger.

When the nine-year-old Gobind held his father's severed head in his hands, he was only too aware of his unique heritage: fearless martyrdom to defend the essential rights to life and belief. He also knew how he would carry this legacy forward: injustice and cruelty had to be given an appropriate response. As Cunningham wrote: 'He resolved upon awakening his followers to a new life and upon giving precision and aim to the broad and general institutions of Nanak. In the heart of a powerful empire he set himself the task of subverting it, and from the midst of social degradation and religious corruption he called up the simplicity of manners, singleness of purpose, and enthusiasm of desire.'[3]

Those early years at Anandpur were years of preparation—both martial and spiritual. The grief at Tegh Bahadur's death gradually gave way to an enthusiasm for the tenth Guru who had grown into a sharp-featured, tall and wiry man, handsomely dressed and impressively armed. Anandpur turned into the birthplace of a new nation. It began to see martial exercises and sports—horse racing, musket shooting, archery and swordsmanship. A huge war drum, known as the Ranjit Nagara, was built and installed; its booming beat announced a hunt or a mealtime in the communal kitchen.

At the same time, the Guru, with his amazing talents, concentrated on literary and spiritual acquisitions. He learned Persian, Arabic, Sanskrit, Braj and Avadhi, and studied the ancient classics and texts. His poetic genius was to result in a cornucopia of

---

[3]J.D. Cunningham, *A History of the Sikhs* (1849).

highly accomplished literary work, beginning with *Chandi di Var*, a virile ballad replete with vivid imagery that depicts the contest between gods and demons in inspiring martial rhythm. This would be followed by several major works marked by spiritual depth and artistic beauty—*Jaap Sahib*, *Sudha Sawaiye* (psalms), *Akal Ustat* and *Shabad Hazare* (Songs of Divine praise), *Bachitra Natak* (an autobiography), *Chaubis Avtar*, *Chandi Charitra* and many others, including the *Zafarnama*, collected in the *Dasam Granth*, a text distinct from the Adi Granth. One of the abiding elements of his poetry and philosophy was the metaphor of the sword, the symbol of Shakti, of Durga, indeed of God Himself. The sword was not a weapon of aggression but of righteous action to preserve truth and virtue; in truth, it was more a shield than a sword. This was the sacrament of steel, true and uncompromising, that would weld a new and fearless nation from a passive and demoralized mass.

The Rajput rajas of the surrounding hills watched Guru Gobind Singh's growing influence with consternation. It was not only the splendour of his court that disturbed them but also the casteless nature of the community that he was nurturing, which they saw as a challenge to their time-honoured feudal systems. They also saw the Guru's education, martial training and patronage of the arts as attempts to equate himself with Rajput rulers. The first challenge came from Raja Bhim Chand of Bilaspur (or Kahlur) who demanded that the Guru hand over a richly embroidered canopy and a well-trained elephant. When rebuffed, he had to be persuaded by his fellow rajas not to go to war with the Guru; the truce, however, would prove to be temporary.

One of the hill rajas, Raja Medini Prakash of Sirmur, differed from his clansmen and made friendly overtures towards Guru Gobind Singh. Finally, in 1685, the Guru accepted his invitation to visit Nahan, the picturesque capital of Sirmur. There he was warmly received and spent several days in discourse and in hunting game in the surrounding jungles. While out on the chase one day, he was captivated by the scenic beauty of a spot beside the Yamuna, a few miles below the spur of Nahan. The Guru decided to set camp here and named the place Paonta, after the *pav* or foot that his favourite horse had implanted on the soil. Today a serene gurudwara stands on the banks of the river at the same spot.

The years at Paonta were to be the most creative of his life. He devoted himself to his favourite outdoor activities with his followers and contemplated deeply on the state of the nation and the challenge of reviving the human spirit. He also produced supremely sublime poetry that sang praises of the Almighty and aimed to infuse a new spirit into the populace. A number of poets from all over the country—his poetic court included fifty-two—gathered about him and their creative activity turned Paonta into a cultural and spiritual centre. Sikh lore has it that one day the poets complained to the Guru that the noisy river disturbed their concentration and it is in accordance with the Guru's command that the Yamuna at that spot flows soundlessly to this day.

The huge amount of literature produced at Paonta, along with translations of ancient Sanskrit texts—including the Mahabharata, Puranas and Niti Shastra—into Punjabi and Braj were compiled into a massive anthology called *Vidyasagar*. This huge exercise had a purpose: to bring about a renaissance of ancient knowledge and thus facilitate a spiritual awakening by making the people aware of a heritage they could be proud of, and for this it was necessary through translation to take these texts from the obscure and self-serving possession of the priests and render them comprehensible to the masses. Unfortunately, this valuable compilation itself was lost later during the crossing of the Sirsa river in flood after the evacuation of Anandpur; some of the translations survived through copies made outside the *Vidyasagar* collection.

The tranquil life at Paonta was brought to an end by the hill rajas who had amassed an army headed by Bhim Chand Kahluria and Raja Fateh Shah of Srinagar to challenge the Guru. The two armies met at the field of Bhangani, six miles from Paonta on 22 September 1688. Guru Gobind Singh suffered early setbacks as five hundred Pathans who had been commended to his army by a Muslim divine and follower, Pir Buddhu Shah, broke their loyalty and moved over to the other side. Buddhu Shah then joined the Guru with his four sons and seven hundred followers. The Guru's followers, though not professional soldiers, fought with tremendous spirit and resolute determination. The Guru himself took the field and confronted the brave hill chief and ace marksman, Hari Chand Handuria. With Hari Chand's death, the victory at Bhangani belonged to the Guru and his followers, a decisive demonstration that they could not be trifled with. Guru Gobind Singh was to later describe Bhangani as a 'purposeless' battle that had been foisted upon him.

Anticipating that other battles would follow, the Guru returned to Anandpur and began the building of defensive fortifications. The forts of Anandgarh, Fatehgarh, Lohgarh and Keshgarh were built on strategic natural features. Sure enough, fresh challenges presented themselves. Raja Bhim Chand, the treacherous hill raja who had ironically made his peace with the Guru now sought his assistance to challenge the Mughal commander from Jammu, Alif Khan, who had been sent to enforce tribute from the recalcitrant hill rajas. In a quick and decisive action at Nadaun on the Beas river, Alif Khan was defeated with the help of the Sikhs.

But this victory would have repercussions. The news from Nadaun and the growing strength of Guru Gobind Singh reached Aurangzeb in the Deccan. Incensed, he issued a royal edict in November 1693 preventing the Guru from gathering his followers. This had little effect on Anandpur. Guru Gobind Singh sent out word that his followers should come to celebrate Baisakhi at Anandpur and that they should travel armed, their hair and beards unshorn, so as to openly announce their identities. Mughal pickets guarded the paths but, refusing to be daunted, the Sikhs gathered in strength at Anandpur in March 1694. Baisakhi was celebrated with great fanfare. As was only to be expected, news of this defiance too reached the emperor in the Deccan.

Several attempts at subduing the Sikhs followed. First, Dilawar Khan, the provincial Mughal chief from Kangra, sent a force under his son to surprise the Sikhs but when the Mughal army reached Anandpur in the dark of the night it was taken aback by the stentorian war cries of the defenders and the booming beat of the Ranjit Nagara. Unnerved by the ready response, the Mughals deserted the field. Another expedition under the commander Husain Khan, aided by the duplicitous Bhim Chand, set course for Anandpur but were diverted with a dispute with Raja Gopal of Guler. In the battle that ensued, the Guler chief was victorious with the help of a small body of Sikhs. A livid Aurangzeb then sent an expedition under his son Muazzam, who was to later succeed him to the throne as Bahadur Shah. The commander of the prince's army, Mirza Beg, exacted a heavy toll from the hill rajas but they decided to leave the Guru alone, probably due to the intervention of the poet Bhai Nand Lal who was a devotee of the Guru and had also served as secretary to Prince Muazzam.

These clashes finally gave way to a few years of peace and the Guru devoted these to contemplation and literary activity. He completed the autobiographical *Bachitra Natak* and supervised the translation of the Upanishads and other classical texts. He also turned his attention to the organizational structure of the Sikh communities. A fundamental change was made by the abolition of the institution of *masands* (officials appointed to administer the far-flung congregations) that dated back to the time of Guru Amar Das. The *masands* had become corrupt, divisive and venal. Once freed of their tyranny and corrupt practices, the congregations established a direct link with Anandpur. The time was now ripe for the most dramatic transformation of the community.

The Baisakhi festival of 1699 arrived in an atmosphere of high expectation. A special command had gone out to the congregations to gather in large numbers at Anandpur. About eighty thousand followers gathered to celebrate the festival with a meditative Guru Gobind Singh. When the Guru appeared before the gathering he most unexpectedly drew his sword and demanded that one person come forth from the congregation and sacrifice his head for the sake of the faith. The audience was dumbfounded; the Guru seemed to have lost his mind. Some left in panic but the majority sat quietly. Finally, a man called Daya Ram came forward and offered his head. The Guru took him into tent and came back, his sword dripping with blood. The call for sacrifice was repeated another four times and four men—Dharam Das, Mohkam Chand, Himmat Rai and Sahib Chand—came forward in response to the call of the Guru and were similarly 'sacrificed'. According to some versions, the blood on the sword is believed to be that of slaughtered goats.

After this unprecedented turn of events, the Guru brought back the five men from the tent, dressed in new robes with turbans on their heads. These men were to be the *panj pyaras* or the five beloved ones. They had overcome the most debilitating of enemies—fear. They would form the core of the order of the Khalsa, or the Pure, which was about to be born. Guru Gobind then performed the simple yet immensely significant ceremony of baptism. He poured clean water into an iron bowl, added sugar to it, and stirred it with a double-edged dagger as he recited verses from the sacred writings. Thus, with the combination of sweetness and steel was prepared amrit—or ambrosia—which was administered to each of the five Sikhs by the Guru with a rousing cry of *Sri Waheguru ji ka Khalsa, Sri Wahegure ji ki Fateh* (The Khalsa belongs to the Glorious God; and the Glorious God is Victorious). The rallying cry remains with the Sikhs to this day.

The baptism was a rebirth for the five into a new family, a casteless brotherhood of inspired belief. It was the end of the debilitating boundaries of their caste, their creed and ritual. Each one of them was to henceforth carry the surname Singh, or Lion, and to carry the five emblems of the brotherhood. These are the five Ks of Sikhism: *kesh*, or unshorn hair and beard; a *kangha*, or comb to keep the hair tidy; *kara*, a steel bracelet ; *kachh*, short breaches in keeping with the demands of soldiering; and *kirpan*, a sword. In another unexpected move, the Guru then asked the *panj pyaras* to baptize him in the same manner as he had baptized them. He was not to be their superior but was to be merged into the brotherhood. The Guru was not only the Guru but the disciple too; the brotherhood of saint-soldiers, ready to die for the righteous cause, was created in his image and became his alter ego.

The creation of the Khalsa was the apogee of the work started two centuries earlier by Guru Nanak. The martial elements infused by the tenth Guru were to be tempered by the strong spiritual context created by the combined teachings of all the Gurus. Strength was to be exercised for the right cause and never for aggrandizement or aggression. The community was inspired by belief in the One God and preached the equality of man; its preferred action was the amelioration of man's condition in relation to society rather than individual piety or asceticism. Ritualism and idolatry were denounced; the congregation and community were promoted as an important part of life. The Khalsa was to hold the sword in one hand and the rosary in the other.

The Guru's message to the initiates was clear: 'You will love man as man, making no distinction of caste or creed . . . You will only bow your heads to your Master. You will never worship stock, stone, idol or tomb. Remember always, in times of danger or difficulty, the names of the masters: Nanak, Angad, Amar Das, Ram Das, Arjan Dev, Hargobind Sahib, Har Rai Sahib, Har Krishan, Tegh Bahadur. I make you a rosary of these names and you shall not pray each for himself, but for the entire Khalsa. In each of you the whole brotherhood shall be incarnated. You are my sons, both in flesh and spirit.' With this inspired and creative act, Guru Gobind Singh started a new era, an age of chivalry and gallantry in which ordinary and suppressed people would become stout-hearted saint-soldiers, crusaders against oppression. He had taught the sparrows to hunt the hawks.

But the going would not be smooth. The hill rajas, whom the Guru invited to join his growing community at Anandpur, refused to do so. In a petition sent to Delhi they vented their jealousy at his growing influence: 'The Guru has established a new sect distinct from the Hindus and the Muhammadans, to which he has given the name of Khalsa. He has united the four castes into one, and made many followers . . . He suggested to us that if we rose in rebellion against the emperor, he would assist us with all his forces, because the emperor had killed his father, and he desired to avenge his death . . . We cannot restrain him and have accordingly come to crave the protection of this just government against him . . . Should you delay to punish and restrain him, his next expedition will be against the capital of your empire.'

In response, Aurangzeb, still in the Deccan, dispatched two Mughal commanders, Painda Khan and Din Beg, to deal with the Sikhs. Aided by the hill rajas, the Mughal forces joined battle with the small but determined band of Sikhs. Painda Khan was killed by Guru Gobind Singh in single combat and the Mughal army was routed. The hill rajas fled the battlefield only to regroup after a while and lay siege to Anandpur. Once again, the siege had to be lifted in the face of stiff resistance. Several such skirmishes followed over the next three years but the Sikh community at Anandpur held fast. Finally, in the winter of 1704, the largest ever combined force of the Mughals and the hill rajas that had ever been put together descended upon Anandpur only to be met by a determined, planned and aggressive response. When several bloody battles only resulted in huge losses for the attacking army, they settled down to a comprehensive siege. All food supplies were cut off and even a hill stream that used to supply water to Anandpur was diverted.

Despite brave, lightning strikes by the Sikhs for the replenishment of supplies, the situation inside the city gradually worsened. Messages came from Aurangzeb, authenticated by vows on the Quran, assuring safe passage for the Guru and his entourage if he evacuated Anandpur. Ultimately, not willing to subject his loved ones to starvation, the Guru decided to leave. His party consisted of his mother, Mata Gujri, his two wives and four sons along with about five hundred Sikhs.

The royal promise, of course, was only made to be broken; the Guru's party was attacked as they reached the banks of the flooded Sirsa river. Ude Singh, one of the Guru's most skilful commanders mounted a rearguard action—and died in the process—to allow the others to ford the river. Several Sikhs died in the chilly waters and the party was dispersed in the confusion of pursuit. Mata Gujri, the Guru's mother, along with his two younger sons, Zorawar Singh and Fateh Singh, were escorted by an old retainer, Gangu, to his village; the two wives were escorted to Delhi. The Guru was left with his two elder sons, Ajit Singh and Jujhar Singh, and a band of forty Sikhs. Pursued by a reinforced Mughal army he reached a small mud fortress in the village of Chamkaur.

Here, on 22 December 1704, was to be fought a battle rare in the chronicles of gallantry. The Sikhs came out in batches of five to meet the huge pursuing army and each man fought his way to a brave death. Both sons of the Guru, Ajit and Jujhar, as well as two of the original *panj pyaras*, Mohkam Singh and Himmat Singh, were killed in hand-to-hand combat after causing havoc in the Mughal ranks. At the end of the day the Guru was left with only five Sikhs. They entreated him to escape, saying that if he lived the Khalsa would flourish. Presented with the command of the five Sikhs, Guru Gobind Singh left the fortress, extinguishing the night torches of the enemy even as he left. Three of the Sikhs were to ultimately catch up with him while the remaining two would continue to battle till their last breath.

The Guru roamed alone in the wintry nights in the forest of Macchiwara, without food or shelter. It was in this state that he composed the heart-rending verses of *Mittar Piare nu*.

Tell the Beloved Friend of the condition of his followers:

Without Him, the comfort of soft beds is a plague,
Life in palaces may well be a serpent,

The jug of wine is a cross, the cup a dagger;
Without Him, life is a butcher's knife itself.

The rough dwelling of a friend is welcome,
And hell itself to live the life of the rich.

Finally, reunited with his three companions from Chamkaur and aided by two friendly Pathans, Guru Gobind Singh wended his way through searching enemy patrols and reached the village of Jatpura where he learned of the fate that had befallen his mother and two younger sons. The servant Gangu had betrayed them and handed them over to Nawab Wazir Khan of Sarhind. The nawab offered the two young boys, aged eight and six, blandishments to convert them to Islam. When they adamantly and fearlessly refused, they were bricked alive. (Some chroniclers believe that they were extricated from the wall and then put to death by the sword.) Mata Gujri died of shock when she heard the news. The nawab of Malerkotla intervened unsuccessfully with Wazir Khan to spare the lives of the boys. Malerkotla has since enjoyed a unique place in Sikh lore and has become synonymous with inter-communal harmony. Even during the bloody communal riots that marked the Partition of India, no Muslim was harmed in Malerkotla.

The Guru received the horrible news with equanimity and fell into prayer, thanking the Almighty for giving him the opportunity to render to Him what belonged to Him. He then proceeded to the village of Dina. Here he received from Aurangzeb a conciliatory message inviting him to meet him in the Deccan. While historians differ on exact details of the sequence, it is generally believed that this message was in response to a letter written to the emperor by the Guru after Chamkaur, a letter titled *Fatehnama*. The Guru now responded with the *Zafarnama* and dispatched it to the Deccan with two Sikhs, Daya Singh and Dharam Singh. Aurangzeb, according to the version of traditional Sikh chroniclers, was so moved by the letter and impressed with its forthright fearlessness that even as he lay sick in bed, he dictated a letter to his wazir in the north, Munim Khan, to show friendship towards Guru Gobind Singh and invite him to meet the emperor. The letter was sent to Delhi in the hands of the emperor's mace-bearer Muhammed Beg, accompanied by the two Sikh messengers.

While all this was happening, the Guru had moved on to Khidrana which housed the only reservoir in the area. Here a pitched battle was fought with the forces of Wazir Khan, the nawab of Sarhind. A small band of forty Sikhs fought to their death. They were from among those who had deserted the Guru during the siege of Anandpur and now sought redemption by laying down their lives. The daily Sikh prayer or *Ardas* remembers them as the forty 'saved ones' (*muktas*). The spot of the battle has since been known as Muktsar or the Pool of Salvation.

Guru Gobind then continued his travels through the Malwa area of Punjab. This was then a rather thinly populated area, still very much a scrubland and jungle with agricultural settlement confined to the banks of the rivers. Here he began to revitalize the people with his presence and teachings. A large number of the peasants came under his influence and the Sikh faith took firm roots in the area. Finally, he took off his armour at a spot near Talwandi Sabo and rested. This place became known as Damdama, or the place of repose. During his nine-month stay here, thousands of people took the baptism of the double-edged dagger. It was here too that the Guru, with the help of his confidant, the scholarly Bhai Mani Singh, put together the authorized version of the Adi Granth. To the first version of the Granth that had been put together by Guru Arjan were added the hymns of the ninth Guru, Tegh Bahadur. His own writings would later be put together after his death by Bhai Mani Singh in the *Dasam Granth*. Damdama became a gathering point for scholars and poets and the Guru likened the place to Kashi (Varanasi) as a centre of learning; subsequently, Damdama developed a strong tradition for scholarship and calligraphy.

Leaving behind the tranquility of Damdama, the Guru set out again. While historians again differ on the purpose of the journey, it seems probable that the Guru had not heard of the impact that the *Zafarnama* had had on the emperor, and the air being rife with rumours of the failing health of the ninety-year-old Aurangzeb, he set out to seek a meeting. When he reached Rajputana in February 1707, however, he received news that the emperor had died in Ahmednagar.

A war of succession immediately broke out among the Mughal princes. The eldest, Muazzam Shah, known to be a liberal man, sought assistance from Guru Gobind Singh. The Guru recalled that Muazzam had earlier ignored his father's dictate to wage war on the Sikhs. A detachment of Sikh soldiers aided Muazzam in his battle against his rival Azam Shah in June 1707, and as a result of the victory, Muazzam ascended the throne in Delhi as Bahadur Shah.

A cordial meeting took place between the emperor and the Guru at Agra. All courtesies were extended by the emperor. Guru Gobind then decided to accompany him to the Deccan to quell a rebellion by another prince, wanting to utilize the opportunity to continue the dialogue with the emperor and seek a settlement to the troubles in Punjab. After many conversations, and by the time they reached Nanded, it was obvious that the emperor was not willing to take a real stand on issues such as reining in the hostile Wazir Khan of

Sarhind and curbing the tyranny of the Mughal functionaries. Once again, this is the version of the traditional Sikh chroniclers and little is known from Mughal sources about the discussions.

While in Nanded, the Guru attracted many followers including the ascetic Madho Dass, who would later wreak vengeance on Sarhind as Banda Bahadur. However, Nanded was also to be the scene of tragedy. Disturbed by the possibility of the growing entente between the Guru and the emperor, Nawab Wazir Khan of Sarhind had infiltrated two assassins into the Guru's congregation. One evening, they made their way into the Guru's tent and stabbed him near the heart. Drawing his sword, the Guru killed one of them; the other was beheaded by the Sikhs who rushed in. Although the Guru's wound healed well, it reopened a few days later when he attempted to stretch a powerful bow. On 7 October 1708, Guru Gobind Singh died from excessive bleeding.

Even as he ebbed, the Guru drew upon his tremendous inner strength and gathered his followers around him. He directed them to revere only the Adi Granth after him; the Holy Book would be their Guru and would become known as the Guru Granth Sahib. It contained the spirit of all the Gurus. The Khalsa would be the Guru itself; the Guru had merged into the faith.

In his short span of forty-two years, Guru Gobind Singh had achieved his near impossible mission. Facing personal tragedies with a calm resolve not reserved for ordinary men, he had brought about a miraculous transformation of the spirit of a people, infusing in them a self-belief and spiritual strength with which they could fight oppression and tyranny. He made fearlessness a way of life and righteous valour a philosophy. He was a true saint-soldier whose martial prowess was matched by his spiritual achievement. The *Zafarnama* is a short but powerful example of his forthright, fearless philosophy as well as of his literary poetic genius.

كمالِ كرامات قائم كريم

رضا بخش رازق رهاک و رحيم

Kamaal-e karamat kayam karim
Raza baksh razak rahak o rahim

اماں بخش بخشنده و دستگير

رضا بخش روزی ده و دل پذير

Ama-baksh bakshindeh o dastgir
Raza baksh rozi deh o dilpazir

⚛1⚛

He is the immortal Lord,
Eternal, all powerful
Giver of joy and salvation,
Bountiful and merciful.[1]

⚛2⚛

O Merciful One
Who protects and guides,
O Charming One
Who forgives and provides.

---

[1] Verses 1–12 are in praise of God.

شہنشاہِ خوبی دہ و رہنموں
کہ بیگون بیچوں چوں بے نموں

Shahenshah-e khubi deh o rehnamu
Ki begun bechun chun benamun

نہ ساز و نہ باز و فوج و نہ فرش
خُداوند بخشِندۂ عیش عرش

Na saaz o na baaz o fauj o na farsh
Khudawand bakshindeh aish arsh

Mightiest of emperors,
Giver of good, guide without peer,
Ethereal and formless,
He is unique, beyond compare.

~4~

Without pomp or glory,
Or armies to command,
Giver of pleasures and joy
From His generous hand.

جہاں پاک زبرست ظاہر ظہور

عطا می دہد ہمچو حاضر حضور

Jahan pak zabarast zahir zahur
Ata medehad hamchu hazar hazur

عطا بخش او پاک پروردگار

رحیم است روزی دہ و ہر دیار

Ata baksh o pak parwardigar
Rahimast rozi deh o har diyar

Beyond this world, powerful,
He is manifest all around.
In the gifts that He bestows,
His presence does abound.

~ 6 ~

The Bountiful, the Pure One,
Protects with His hand,
All merciful is He,
The provider, in every land.

که صاحب دیار است اعظم عظیم

که حُسن الجمال است رازق رحیم

Ki sahib dayarast azam azim
Ki husn al-jamal ast razak rahim

که صاحب شعور است عاجز نواز

غریب الپرست و غنیم الگُداز

Ki sahib shaour ast aajiz-nawaz
Garib ul-parast o ganim ul-gudaz

7

The greatest of greats,
Master of every sphere,
Merciful, kind sustainer,
Beauteous beyond compare.

8

The wisest of the wise,
Protector of the weak,
Destroyer of tyrants,
The keeper of the meek.

شریعت پرست و فضیلت مآب

حقیقت شناس و نبی الکتاب

Shariyat parast o fazilat muab
Haqiqat shinas o nabi ul-kitab

کہ دانش پژوہست صاحب شعور

حقیقت شناس است و ظاہر ظہور

Ki danash pazhu ast sahib shaour
Haqiqat shinas ast o zahir zahur

9

The protector of the path,
All virtue rests in His name,
The diviner of the Truth,
Holy books echo his fame.

10

The supreme font of wisdom,
All-knowing and wisest,
The diviner of the Truth,
In everything manifest.

~11~

شناسندهٔ علم و عالم خُدائے

کُشائندهٔ کارِ عالم کُشائے

Shinasindeh-e ilm o alam khudae
Kushaindeh-e kar-e alam kushae

~12~

گذارندهٔ کارِ عالم کبیر

شناسندهٔ علم و عالم امیر

Guzarindeh-e kar-e alam kabir
Shinasindeh-e ilm o alam amir

⟡11⟡

The Lord of all creation,
Master of all wisdom,
He resolves all problems
Of His eternal kingdom.

⟡12⟡

He is the Almighty,
All creation at His call;
He is all-knowing,
The Master of all.

داستان

Dastaan

~13~

مرا اعتبارِ بریں قسم نیست

کہ ایزد گواہ است یزداں یکیست

Ma-ra itibar-e bar een qasam nest

Ki eizad gawah ast yazdan yakest

~14~

نہ قطرہ مرا اعتبار بروست

کہ بخشی و دیواں ہمہ کذب گوست

Na katra ma-ra itibar-e bar o ast

Ki bakshi o diwan hama kizabgo ast

The Tale

~13~

I have no faith at all
In the oath that you swear,
That the God who is One
Your witness does bear.

~14~

Not a jot of trust
Do I now have in you,
Whose generals and ministers
Are all liars, untrue.

~15~

کسے قول قرآں کند اعتبار

ہماں روز آخر شود مرد خوار

Kase qoul-e Quran kunad itibar
Haman roz aakhir shavad mard khwar

~16~

ہُما را کسے سایہ آید بہ زیر

برو دست دارد نہ زاغ دلیر

Huma ra kase saaye aayad bazer
Bar o dast darad na zaag-e daler

Such oaths on the Quran
Whosoever does believe,
Will be wretched at the end,
Destroyed, beyond reprieve.

➤16➤

The one touched by Huma's[2] shadow
And taken under its wing
Is beyond harm from clever crows,
Their designs mean nothing.

---

[2] Huma is the mythological and legendary bird whose touch or shadow is said to be auspicious.

❦17❦

کسے پُشت اُفتد پسِ شیرِ نر

نہ گرد بُز و میش و آہو گذر

Kase pusht uftad pase sher nar
Na gird buz o mesh o aahu guzar

❦18❦

قسم مُصحف خدع گر ایں خرام

نہ فوج عزیزم را سم افغنام

Qasam mushaf-e khadeh gar een khoram[3]
Na fauj-e azizam ra sum afganam

---

[3] Multiple readings exist of this verse; in all likelihood a distortion has crept into the text, making it difficult to untangle.

As one protected by the lion
Is set free from all fear,
He cannot then be harmed
By goats, sheep and deer.

~18~

In your false oath on the Quran
Had I not believed,
My brave army wouldn't be crippled,
Nor in such manner deceived.

گرسنہ چہ کارے کند چہل نر

کہ دَہ لک برآید برو بے خبر

Guresneh chi kare kunad chehel nar
Ki dah lak barayad bar o bekhabar

کہ پیماں شِکن بیدرنگ آمدند

میان تیغ تیر و تفنگ آمدند

Ki paiman shikan bedarang aamdand
Miyan tegh teer o tufang aamdand

19

Forty brave but hungry men
How are they expected to defend
When countless enemy hordes
Upon them suddenly descend?

20

All of a sudden they descended,
Giving the lie to their words,
Brandishing their guns,
Raining arrows, waving swords.

به لاچارگی درمیاں آمدم

به تدبیر تیر و تفنگ آمدم

Ba lacharegi darmiyan aamdam
Ba tadbir teer o tufang aamdam

چوں کار از ہمہ حیلتے در گذشت

حلال است بُردن به شمشیر دست

Chun kar az hameh heelate dar guzasht
Halal ast burdan bi-shamsher dast

21

Then left with no choice
I joined battle with your hordes,
Came with much deliberation
Amidst the arrows and swords.

22

When all has been tried, yet
Justice is not in sight,
It is then right to pick up the sword,
It is then right to fight.

~23~

چه قسم قرآں من کنم اعتبار

وگر نه تو گوئی من ایں ره چکار

Chi qasme Quran man kunam itibar
Vagarnah tu goi man een rah chi kar

~24~

نه دانم که ایں مرد روباه پیچ

دگر هرگز ایں ره نیاید به هیچ

Na danam ki een mard robah-e pech
Digar hargiz een rah niayad bahech

Why should I then believe
In oaths on the Holy Word?
If I had not been deceived,
Would I go down this road?

I had no knowledge
Of this man's wily heart,
Else, I would not have trusted
Or come down this path.[4]

---

[4] This verse has been subject to several interpretations.

هر آنکس که قولِ قرآں آیدش
نزد بستن و کشتن و بایدش

Haran kas ki qoul-e Quran aayedash
Nazad bastan o kushtan o bayadash

برنگِ مگس سیه پوش آمدند
به یکبارگی در خروش آمدند

Ba rang-e magas siyaposh aamdand
Ba yak baregi dar kharosh aamdand

~25~

Every single trusting soul who
In your oath on the Quran believed,
Should not have come to any harm,
Nor killed, nor captured, nor deceived.

~26~

Your men all clad in black
Swarmed upon us like flies;
Of a sudden they descended,
The battlefield echoed their cries.

～27～

هر آں کس ز دِیوار آمد بیروں

بخوردن یکے تیر شُد غرق خُوں

Haran kas ze deewar aamad birun
Bakhurdan yake teer shod garq-e khun

～28～

کہ بیروں نیامد کسے زاں دیوار

نخوردند تیر و نگشتند خوار

Ki birun niamad kase zan deewar
Na khurdand teer o na gushtand khwar

Each of your men who stepped
Beyond the sheltering wall,
Got an arrow through his heart,
And then bleeding did fall.

Those who hid behind the wall
And escaped the strife,
Were safe from our arrows,
Held on to dear life.

چو دیدم کہ ناہر بیامد بجنگ

چشیدہ یکے تیرمن بیدرنگ

Chun deedam ki Nahar biamad be jung
Chashideh yak e teer-e man bedarang

ہمآخر گریزند بجاۓ مصاف

بسے خان خوردند بیروں گزاف

Ham akhir gurezand bajaye musaf
Base khan khurdand birun gazaf

I saw then the proud Nahar
Swagger upon the battlefield;
Forthwith he tasted my arrow,
And his soul he did yield.

Then many arrogant Khans
Who had boasted long and loud,
Deserted they the battlefield
Under the shadow of a shroud.

کہ افغانِ دیگر بیامد بہ جنگ

چُوں سَیلِ رواں ہمچو تیر و تفنگ

Ki Afghan digar biamad be jung[5]
Chun saile rawan humchu teer o tufang

بسے حملہ کردند بہ مردانگی

ہم از ہوشگی ہم ز دیوانگی

Base hamleh kardand ba mardangi
Hum az hoshgi hum ze diwangi

---

[5] In verses 31–32, grammar makes it difficult to decide whether they refer to a single Afghan warrior or a group of Afghan soldiers. While one would expect a large group to charge the fort, the heroic mode of the Chamkaur battle would also allow one warrior to come forth to do battle alone.

Another charging Afghan horde
Then loomed into sight,
Rising like a river in flood,
A gun shot, an arrow in flight.

The Afghan fought hard,
Attacking from right and left,
At times with a clever plan
But often of wisdom bereft.

❦33❦

بسے حملہ کرد و بسے زخم خورد

دوکس را بجاں کشت وہم جاں سُپرد

Base hamleh kard o base zakhm khurd

Do kas ra bajaan kusht v hum jaan sapurd

❦34❦

کہ آں خواجۂ مردودِ سایۂ دیوار

بمیداں نیامد بمردانہ وار

Ki aan Khwaja mardud saaye deewar

Be maidan niamad ba mardana var

34   *Guru Gobind Singh*

~33~

Many a time did he attack,
Suffered many wounds in strife;
He killed two of my brave men
Then lay down his own life.

~34~

But your cowardly Khwaja chief
Hid behind the sheltering wall,
Too scared to fight like a man,
Did not enter the battle at all.

دریغا! اگر رُوئے اُو دیدے

بیک تیر لاچار بخشیدے

Darega! Agar roo-ye o deedam-e
Ba yak teer lachar bakhsheedam-e

ہم آخر بے زخم تیر و تفنگ

دوسوئے بے کشتہ شد بید رنگ

Ham akhir base zakhm teer o tufang
Do su-ye base kushte shod bedarang

Alas! Had the coward stepped out,
Had I once seen his face,
My single arrow would have ensured
A quick end to his days.

~36~

From flying bullets and arrows
Profusely the wounded bled,
Until finally, on that battlefield,
Many of both sides lay dead.

بسے بار بارید تیر و تفنگ
زمیں گشت ہمچوں گلِ لالہٴ رنگ

Base bar bareed teer o tufang
Zameen gasht humchun gul-e laleh rang

سر و پائے انبوہ چنداں شُدہ
کہ میداں پُر از گوئے چوگاں شدہ

Sar o paa-ye amboh chanda shudeh
Ki maidan pur az goye chaugan shudeh

Under the shower of bullets and arrows
So numerous were the dead,
That like the poppy flower
The earth itself turned red.

Chopped heads and hacked limbs
Lay piled on the battlefield,
As if they were only balls
And sticks on some polo field.

ترکار تیر و ترنکار کماں

برآمد یکے ہاے ہُو از جہاں

Tarkaar teer o tarankar kamaan
Baramad yake hai hu az jahan

دگر شورشِ کیبرِ کینۂ کوش

زمردانِ مرداں بیروں رفت ہوش

Digar shorish-e kaibar-e keeneh kosh
Ze mardaan-e mardan birun raft hosh

So fearsome the scream of arrows
So awesome the twang of bows,
That from a cowering world
A loud cry at once arose.

≈40≈

The screaming arrows rained death,
Each one to its target sped,
And the bravest of your men
Were counted among the dead.

ہم آخر چہ مردی کند کارزار

کہ بر چہل تن آیدش بے شمار

Ham akhir chi mardi kunad karzar
Ki bar chahal tan aayedash beshumar.

چراغ جہاں چوں شدہ برقع پوش

شاہِ شب برآمد ہمہ جلوہ جوش

Chirag-e jahan chun shudeh burqaposh
Shah-e shab baramad hameh jalwa josh

~41~

But how long can forty men,
Even the bravest of brave,
Stave off a countless horde
Charging in an endless wave?

~42~

When the light of the world
Drew a veil across his face,
The king of the night rose
In all his beauty and grace.

43

هر آنکس که قول قرآں آیدش
که یزداں بر او رهنما آیدش

Har aan kas ki qoul-e Quran aayedash
Ki yazdan bar o rehnuma aayedash

44

نه پیچیده موئے نه رنجیده تن
که بیروں خود آورد دشمن شِکن

Na pecheed mu-ye na ranjeed tan
Ki berun khud aawurd dushman shikan

44   *Guru Gobind Singh*

43

If one believes in a promise
Sworn on the Holy Word,
Then he is safe from all harm
He is guided by the Lord.

44

Thus guided by God himself
And protected by His grace,
He emerges, unscathed, unharmed,
From the enemy's foul embrace.

نددانم که این مرد پیماں شکن
که دولت پرستست ایماں فِگن

Na danam ki een marad paiman shikan
Ki daulat parast ast iman figan

نه ایماں پرستی نه اوضاع دیں
نه صاحب شناسی نه محمّد یقیں

Na iman parasti na auza-e din
Na sahib shinashi na Mehmad yakin

Unaware was I that this perjurer
Worshipped no God but gold;
His faith he had flung aside,
His rotten soul he had sold.[6]

∼46∼

There is no belief in religion,
And faith is discarded,
The Lord is ignored,
The Prophet disregarded.

---

[6] Some commentators believe, contrary to traditional interpretation, that the promise-breaker in this and some other verses is not Aurangzeb but the local Mughal commander.

ہر آنکس کہ ایماں پرستی کند

نہ پیماں خودش پیش و پستی کند

Har aan kas ki iman parasti kunad
Na paiman khudash pesh o pasti kunad

کہ ایں مرد را ذرہ اعتبار نیست

چہ قسم قرآں است یزداں یکیست

Ki een marad ra zareh itibar nest
Chi qasm-e Quran ast yazdan yakest

～47～

Those who are firm of faith
And true believers of God,
Break not their promises thus
But stay firm to their word.

～48～

There can be no trust in a man who
Swears on the Quran and One God,
But values not the holy oath
And is false to his given word.

چوقسم قرآں صد کند گند اختیار

مرا قطره ناید از و اعتبار

Chun qasm-e Quran sad kunad ikhtiar
Ma-ra katre naayad az o itibar

اگرچہ ترا اعتبار آمدے

کمر بستہ پیشواز آمدے

Agarche to-ra itibar aamd-e
Kamar bastahe peshwaz aamd-e

And now even a hundred times
If on the Quran were he to swear,
His word I would never believe,
For his promises I do not care.

If I had truly believed
In your promise, in your oath,
To greet your message I would
With ceremony come forth.[7]

---

[7] Again, this verse has varying interpretations; some traditional
commentators have read this to mean: 'If you, the emperor, had faith in your
oath, then you would have come forward yourself.'

کہ فرصت بر سر ترا ایں سخن

کہ قول خدا است قسم است من

Ki farz ast bar sar to-ra een sukhan
Ki qoul-e khuda ast qasam ast man

اگر حضرتِ خود ستادہ شود

بجاں و دِلے کار واضح شود

Agar hazrat-e khud sitadeh shavad
Ba jaan-o dile kar vazeh shavad

And now it is your duty
Imposed by your word,
You have sworn to keep
Your oath on your God.

In fact if Your Majesty
Had been present here,
All that has transpired
Would have been clear.

~53~

شمارا چو فرض است کارے کنی

بموجب نوشته شمارے کنی

Shuma ra chu farz ast kare kuni
Bamujab navishteh shumare kuni

~54~

نوشته رسید و بگفتِ زباں

باید که ایں کار به راحت رساں

Navishteh rasid o ba gufteh zuban
Babayad ki een kar ba rahat rasan

It remains your burden
In such a manner to act,
That your act be in keeping
With your written pact.

Your oral word I have received,
The written too is in my possession,
Now this task should be done
So that it gives satisfaction.

هموں مرد باید شود سخنور

نہ شکم دِگر در دہان دِگر

Hamun mard bayad shavad sukhanwar
Na shikm-e digar dar dahan-e digar

کہ قاضی مرا گفتِ بیروں نئیم

اگر راستی خود بیاری قدم

Ki qazi ma-ra gufteh berun nayam
Agar rasti khud biyari qadam

Men must speak the truth,
The truth living in their thoughts,
Not have a promise on their lips
And a lie in their hearts.

To what your qazi has said
I am still ready to agree;
If your intentions are clear
Then you should come to me.[8]

---

[8] A qazi had delivered to Guru Gobind Singh the oath sworn by the emperor on the Holy Quran, along with an oral message. The essence of the message conveyed the high respect in which the emperor held the Guru. The emperor expressed a desire to come and meet the Guru and address all grievances once he was free from his preoccupations with campaigns in the Deccan. Meanwhile he promised safe passage if the Guru with his family and men left the Anandpur fort that was under long siege by the Mughals. This was the promise that was promptly broken by the Mughal commanders.

خرا گر ببايد آں قولِ قرآں

بہ نزدِ شما را رسانم ساں

To-ra gar babayad aan qoul-e Quran

Ba nazd-e shuma ra rasanam haman

کہ تشریف در قصبۂ کانگڑ کند

وزاں پس ملاقات باہم شود

Ki tashrif dar qasbeh Kangar kunad

Vazan pas mulaqat baham shavad

If you need to see that oath
Sworn on the Holy Book,
I can have it sent forthwith
For you to take another look.[9]

If here to Kangar village
You were to proceed,
We could meet face-to-face
To talk of word and deed.[10]

---

[9] This could either imply the Quran itself on which the oath was inscribed or a royal missive containing the message sworn on the Quran.

[10] The textual problems and multiple interpretations are perhaps most pronounced in verses 58–61. Traditionally these are seen as an invitation by the Guru to the emperor to come and meet him in the Malwa region of the Punjab. He was willing to be reassured by the emperor that the latter was true to his oath on the Quran, that the promise was broken only by local commanders who would be punished and justice be done.

Contrarily, some later commentators have suggested that these verses in fact quote the emperor inviting the Guru to come and meet him. Perhaps because of these contradictions and difficulties in reconciliation, verse 61–63 are omitted in some versions.

نہ ذرّہ دریں راہ خطرہ تُراست

ہمہ قوم بیراڑ حُکمِ مراست

Na zara dar een rah khatra to rast
Hame qaum-e Bairar huqm-e marast

~60~

بیا تو سُخن خود زُبانی کُنم

بُروئے شُما مہربانی کُنم

Biya ta sukhan[11] khud zubani kunam
Ba ru-ye shuma meherbani kunam

---

[11] In some versions, the word here is '*ba man*'; but '*sukhan*' seems more appropriate.

~59~

There is no danger to you here,
No one will raise a hand;
This community of Bairars[12]
Is under my command.

~60~

Come so that we can meet
And talk face-to-face,
I can show you forgiveness
And grant you my grace.

---

[12] Traditionally taken to be the Brar jats of Malwa.

~61~

یک اسب شائستہ یک ہزار

بیا تا گیری بہ من ایں دیار

Yake asb shayesteh yak hazaar
Biya ta bagiri ba man een diyar

~62~

شہنشاہ را بندۂ چاکرم

اگر حکم آید بجاں حاضرم

Shahenshah ra banda-e chakram
Agar hukam aayad ba jaan hazram

62   *Guru Gobind Singh*

Present me perhaps a fine horse
That's valued at a thousand,
I may grant you if you seek,
In bounty, this tract of land.[13]

Of the King of Kings
I am but a humble knave;
If He were to command
I would respond as a slave.[14]

---

[13] The Guru is telling the emperor that he should not try to conquer this land but if he comes in peace and makes the traditional offering of a fine horse, it is possible that the Guru would grant him this tract as bounty. Some interpret this as an offer of a thousand-horse rank from the emperor to the Guru.

[14] In some readings the reference here is not to God, but to Aurangzeb, in which case the tone of the verse can be read as ironical.

اگرچہ بیاید بہ فرمانِ من

حضورت بیایم ہمہ جان و تن

Agarche biayad bi farman-e man
Hazoorat biayam hameh jaan o tan

اگر تو بہ یزداں پرستی کنی

بکارِ ما ایں نہ سُستی کنی

Agar tu ba yazdan parasti kuni
Ba kar-e ma een na susti kuni

Even now if a command
Were to be sent to me,
With my body and soul
I would appear before thee.[15]

If you hold your faith dear
And you a true follower be,
Then you should tarry no more
In settling matters with me.

---

[15] As in footnote 14.

بباید که یزداں شناسی کنی

نه گفته کسے کس خراشی کنی

Babayad ki yazdan shinasi kuni

Na gufteh kase kas kharashi kuni

تو مسندنشیں سرورِ کائنات

که عجب است انصاف ایں ہم صفات

Tu masnad nashin sarwar-e kayenat

Ki ajb ast insaf een hum sifat

~65~

You should know the truth
By knowing the True Lord,
And not torment or torture
Based on a casual word.

~66~

You sit on a mighty throne,
You are king of all you survey,
But strange is your justice,
Strange the virtues you display.

~67~

کہ عجب است انصاف و دیں پروری

کہ حیف است صد حیف ایں سروری

Ki ajb ast insaf o din parwari
Ki haif ast sad haif een sarwari

~68~

کہ عجب است عجب است فتوہٴ شما

بجز راستی سخن گفتن زیاں

Ki ajb ast ajb ast fatweh-e shuma
Bajuz rasti sukhan guftan ziyan

68   *Guru Gobind Singh*

Strange are your ways of faith,
Strange the justice you claim,
Shame upon such a rule,
A hundred times, shame!

~68~

Your decrees and commands
Are strange, very strange indeed,
For words shorn of truth
Only to grievous harm lead.

مزاں تیغ بر خونِ کس بے دریغ

تُرا نیز خوں است بہ چرخ تیغ

Mazan tegh bar khun-e kas bedareg
To-ra neez khun ast ba charakh tegh

تو غافل مشو مرد یزداں حراس

کہ او بے نیاز است او بے سپاس

Tu ghafal mashau mard yazdan haraas[16]
Ki o beniaz ast o besapas

---

[16] Here the word '*shinas*' (or 'know') has also been used.

Do not in such heartless manner
Put innocents to the sword,
Else this too shall be your fate
At the hands of the Lord.

🙰70🙰

O God-fearing man
The Lord you must heed,
He is above all flattery,
He is beyond all need.

كه او بے محابست شہنشاہ

زمین و زماں را ہم و پاتشاہ

Ki o bemahab ast shahenshah
Zameen o zaman ra ham o patshah[17]

خداوند ایزد زمین و زماں

کنند است ہر کس مکین و مکاں

Khudawand aizad zameen o zaman
Kunand ast har kas makin o makan

---

[17] Some versions end this line as '*sacha patshah*' or 'true emperor'.

He is the King of Kings,
Truly the Fearless One,
King of the heavens and earth
Master of all Creation.

Supreme Master of all,
From Him Creation takes birth,
Maker of all living beings,
Of the heavens and of earth.

ہم از پیر مورو ہم از پیل تن

کہ عاجز نوازست و غافل شکن

Ham az peer moro ham az peel tan
Ki aajiz-nawaz ast o ghafal-shikan

کہ او را چو اسم است عاجز نواز

کہ او بے سپاس است او بے نیاز

Ki o-ra chu ism ast aajiz-nawaz
Ki o besapas ast o beniaz

The Creator of all creatures:
The elephant strong, the ant weak;
Destroyer of the heedless,
Kind protector of the meek.

Protector of the meek
He is known by that name,
He is beyond all need,
Beyond flattery or fame.

کہ او بے نگوں است او بے چگوں

کہ او رہنما است او رہنموں

Ki o benagun ast o bechagun
Ki o rehnuma ast o rehnamun

کہ برسر تُرا فرض قسم قرآں

بگفتہ شما کار خوبی رساں

Ki bar sar to-ra farz qasm-e Quran
Bigufteh shuma kar khubi rasaan

Unbending, supreme,
He is the Incomparable One;
He shows the right path,
He is the Guiding One.

~76~

The burden of your oath
Lies heavy on your head,
You have to do the right thing
And perform what you've said.

بباید تو دانش پرستی کنی

بکارِ شما چیره دستی کنی

Babayad to danesh parasti kuni
Bi kar-e shuma cheereh dasti kuni

چہ شد کہ چو بچگاں کشتہ چار

کہ باقی بماندست پیچیدہ مار

Chiya shod ki chu bachgan kushteh char
Ki baqi bimand ast pechideh mar.

It is incumbent upon you to act
With wisdom and determination,
Set your hand to the task,
Skilfully take it to resolution.

You killed my four sons:
What difference does that make,
When after their deaths there still
Remains behind a coiled snake?[18]

---

[18] The reference here is to the newly born 'Khalsa' (the Pure) community.

چہ مردی کہ اخگر خموشاں کنی
کہ آتش دماں را بدوراں کنی

Chi mardi ki akhgar khamoshan kuni
Ki aatish daman ra badauran[19] kuni

چہ خوش گفت فردوسی خوش زباں
شتابی بود کارِ آہرمناں

Chi khush guft Firdaus-ye khush zuban
Shitabi buvad kare aaharmanan

---

[19] In some versions the word used here is *'farozan'*.

What sort of manliness is this?
What courage does it require
To stamp out young sparks
And then fan the roaring fire?

The poet Firdausi has said
In words beautiful and chaste,
That they work for the devil
Who act in such unholy haste.[20]

---

[20] Guru Gobind Singh refers here to the summary execution of his two
younger sons at Sarhind.

~81~

کہ ما بارگاہ حضرت آیم شما

ازاں روز باشی و شاہد شما

Ki ma bargah-e hazrat aayam shuma[21]
Azan roz bashi o shahid shuma

~82~

وگر نہ تو ایں ہم فراموش کند

ترا ہم فراموش یزداں کند

Vagarnah to een hum faramosh kunad
To-ra hum faramosh yazdan kunad

---

[21] Multiple interpretations exist of this verse too.

In your Majesty's court
The day I take a stand,
I will be the witness for
The blood on your hand.

~82~

But if you still disregard
Your falsehood and your lies,
You too will be forgotten by God,
Be ever guilty in His eyes.

~83~

اگر کار ایں بر تو بستی کمر

خداوند باشد ترا بہرہ ور

Agar kar een bar to basti kamar
Khudawand bashad to-ra beharavar

~84~

کہ ایں کار نیک است دیں پروری

چو یزداں شناسی بجاں برتری

Ki een kar nek ast din parwari
Chu yazdan shinasi ba jan bartari

But if you set yourself to the task,
And show justice in your ways,
He will still show you mercy
He will forgive you in grace.

Pursuit of truth is worship
It is an act of true piety,
To know the True God
Is life's highest priority.

تُرا من نه دانم که یزداں شناس

برآمد ز تو کارها دلخراش

To-ra man na danam ki yazdan shinas
Baramad zi to kar-ha dil kharash

شناسد همیں تو نه یزداں کریم

نه خواهد همیں تو بدولت عظیم

Shinasad hamin to na yazdan karim
Na khaahad hamin tu badaulat azim

But among those who know God
I do not count your name:
For you have committed only
Acts of infamy and shame.

᠁86᠁

That is why the merciful God
Does not count you in his fold;
He too does not accept you
Despite all your wealth untold.

~87~

اگر صد قرآں را بخوردی قسم

مرا اعتبارے نہ ایں ذرّہ دم

Agar sad Quran ra bakhurdi qasam
Ma-ra itibare na een zareh dam

~88~

حضوری نہ آئم نہ ایں رہ شوم

اگر شہ بخواہد نہ آنجا روم

Hazuri na aayam na een rah shavam
Agar Shah ba khaahad na[22] aanja ravam[23]

---

[22] The word is '*ma*' in some versions.

[23] Grammatical problems and even textual differences make for multiple interpretations. Traditional chroniclers take the reference to Shah to mean God, others take it to mean Prince Muazzam Shah, the emperor's son whom the Guru trusted. The essence of the verse is that the Guru does not trust Aurangzeb's word.

Even if a hundred times
On the Quran you swore,
I would not pay any heed
Or believe you any more.

I will not enter your presence
Nor set foot upon this way,
I would not go there now
If even the prince was to say.

~89~

خوشش شاہِ شاہاں اورنگ زیب

کہ چالاک دستست چابک رکیب

Khushash Shah-e shahan Aurungzeb
Ki chalak dast ast chabuk rakeb

~90~

کہ حسن الجمال است و روشن ضمیر

خُداوندِ مُلک است وصاحب امیر

Ki husn al-jamal ast roshan zameer
Khudawand mulk ast sahib amir

O King of Kings, Aurangzeb,
To your talents too I pay tribute,
You are a horseman of standing
A deft swordsman of repute.[24]

~90~

You are handsome and clever
And steeped in wisdom,
Chief among the chiefs,
Lord of this kingdom.

---

[24] The concluding verses also bring out the virtues and talents of Aurangzeb, often in an ironical tone.

به ترتیب دانش به تدبیر تیغ

خُداوندِ دیگ و خُداوندِ تیغ

Ba tarteeb danesh ba tadbeer tegh

Khudawand-e degh o khudawand-e tegh

که روشن ضمیر است وحُسن الجمال

خُداوندِ بخشندهٔ مُلک و مال

Ki roshan zameer ast husn al-jamal

Khudawand bakhshindeh mulk o mal

Using your wisdom to a plan and
With deliberation your sword,
Of both the sword and bounty,
You have become the lord.

~92~

Blessed by looks and beauty,
Good conscience and high mind,
And of land and wealth
A giver, merciful and kind.

کہ بخشش کبیر است در جنگ کوہ

ملائک صفت چوں ثریا شِکوہ

Ki bakhshish kabir ast dar jung koh
Malayak sift chu suraiya shukoh

شہنشاہ اورنگ زیب عالمیں

کہ دارائے دَور است دُور است دیں

Shahenshah-e Aurungzeb-e aalamin
Ki dara-e daur ast dur ast din

∼93∼

His gifts are truly great,
He is like a rock in war,
He is gifted as the angels,
More glorious than a star.

∼94∼

O King of Kings! The Ornament
That the two worlds does adorn!
The kingdom of the earth is yours,
But not so the heavenly one.

منم کشتنم کوہیاں بُت پرست

کہ آں بُت پرستند من بُت شکست

Manam kushtanam kohiyan but-parast
Ki an but parastand man but-shikast

ببیں گردشِ بے وفائی زماں

پسِ پُشت اُفتد رساند زیاں

Bebin gardish-e bewafai-ye zaman
Pas-e pusht uftad rasanad ziyan

My fight is with the hill princes,
It is them I kill and slay,
For I oppose worship of idols,
And 'tis to idols they pray.

Take a close look also
At this world's faithless way,
When their backs are turned
It does harm to its prey.

بہیں قُدرتِ نیک یزداں پاک

کہ از یک بہ دَہ لک رساند ہلاک

Bebin qudrat-e nek yazdan pak
Ki az yak ba dehlak rasanad halak

~98~

چہ دُشمن کُند مہرباں است دوست

کہ بخشندگی کار بخشندہ اوست

Chi dushman kunad meherban ast dost
Ki bakshindagi kar bakshindeh ost

But take a look too
At the mercy of the Lord,
He blesses a single man
To destroy a countless horde.

~98~

What can the enemy do
When there is such a friend,
The Merciful whose task
Is to give without end.

رہائی دِہ و رہنمائی دِہد

زُباں را بہ صِفتِ آشنائی دِہد

Rahai deh o rehnumai dehad
Zuban ra ba sift aashnai dehad

~100~

خصم را چو کور و کند وقتِ کار

یتیماں بیروں بُرد بزخم خار

Khasam ra chu kor-o kunad waqte kar
Yatiman birun burd be zakhm khar

He delivers and he protects,
He guides to the right way,
And he teaches the tongue
To truly praise and to pray.

The enemy He doesn't spare,
He blinds him in the eye;
The weak and downtrodden
He brings home, safe and dry.

~101~

هرِ آں کس کہ او راستبازی کند

رحیمے برو رحم سازی کند

Har aan kas ki o rastbaazi kunad
Rahim-e bar o rehmsaazi kunad

~102~

کسے خدمت آید بسے دل و جاں

خداوند بخشید بر وے اماں

Kase khidmat aayad base dil o jaan
Khudawand bakhshid bar vai amman

Those who follow the path of truth
In their thought and action,
He showers mercies upon them,
They are granted His compassion.

~102~

Each one who serves Him
With his heart and mind,
Upon him are showered mercies,
True peace he does find.

چی دشمن برآں حیله سازی کند

اگر راہنما بر وے راضی شود

Chi dushman bar an heeleh saazi kunad
Agar rehnuma bar vai raazi shavad

اگر یک بر آید دہ و دہ ہزار

نگہبان او را شود کرد گار

Agar yak bar aayad deh o deh hazaar
Nigehban o-ra shavad kirdgaar

~103~

How can the tricks and plots
Of the enemy ever succeed,
If the Guiding One Himself
With the faithful is pleased?

~104~

Even when upon a lone man
Descend many a thousand,
The Creator protects him,
Shields him with His hand.

ترا گر نظر است لشکر و زر

که ما را نگاه است یزداں شکر

To-ra gar nazar ast lashkar o zar
Ki ma-ra nigah ast yazdan shukar

که اورا غرور است بر ملک و مال

او ما را پناه است یزداں اکال

Ki o-ra gharur ast bar mulk o mal
O ma-ra panah ast yazdan akal

If you gaze with pride
On your armies and gold,
I look unto God
And His mercies untold.

~106~

As you take pride in your wealth
And in the might of your land,
So I trust in the Eternal One,
In the protection of His hand.

تو غافل مشو زیں سپنجی سرائے

کہ عالم بگذرد سرِ جا بجائے

Tu ghafal mashau zeen sepanji sarae
Ki alam biguzrad sar-e ja bajae

ببیں گردش بے وفائی زماں

کہ بگذشت بر ہر مکین و مکاں

Bebin gardish-e bewafai-ye zaman
Ki biguzast bar har makin o makan

Be aware this world is transient,
Here today and tomorrow gone;
The wheel of Time is relentless
It will take us all, one by one.

Beware the unrelenting turn
Of Time's faithless wheel:
It turns for each and every one
It harbours no appeal.

تو بہ جبر عاجز خراشی مکن

قسم را بہ تیشہ تراشی مکن

Tu ba jabr aajiz kharashi makun

Qasam ra ba tesheh tarashi makun

چو حق یار باشد چہ دشمن کند

اگر دشمنی را بصد تن کند

Chu haq yaar bashad chi dushman kunad

Agar dushmani ra ba sad tan kunad

ᐯ109ᐯ

Do not use force unwittingly,
The weak you must spare;
Do not chisel away at oaths,
Be true to the words you swear.

ᐯ110ᐯ

What harm can the enemy do,
If God Himself is a friend,
Though one may be alone
And the enemy becomes a hundred.

خصم دشمنی گر هزار آورد

نه یک موئے او را ازار آورد

Khasam dushmani gar hazaar aaward
Na yak mu-ye o-ra aazar aaward

A thousand plots of the enemy,
Full of treachery and fraud,
They cannot harm a single hair
Of the one protected by God.

IN THE BAZAAR OF LOVE
The Selected Poetry of Amīr Khusrau

Translated by Paul E. Losensky and Sunil Sharma

> *I vow to die*
> *that you might look my way.*
> *See how many have died like me*
> *in the bazaar of love.*

Amīr Khusrau—poet, courtier, mystic, musician—straddled the worlds of politics and religion and helped forge a distinctive synthesis of Muslim and Hindu cultures. His poetry in Persian appealed equally to the Delhi sultans and to his Sufi sheikh, Nizāmuddīn Auliyā. It was appreciated not only in India, where his Hindavi poetry has survived through a lively oral tradition, but also across a cosmopolitan Persianate world that stretched from Turkey to Bengal.

Khusrau's poetry has thrived for centuries and continues to be read and recited to this day. But despite his vast literary output, there is a dearth of translations of his work. *In the Bazaar of Love* offers new translations of Khusrau's poems in Persian and Hindavi, many of which are being translated into English for the first time. Paul Losensky's translations of Khusrau's *ghazals*, including his mystical and romantic poems, comprise fresh renditions of old favourites while also bringing to light several little-known works. Sunil Sharma brings us many of Khusrau's short poems, including those belonging to the *qawwālī* repertoire, as well as a mixed prose-and-verse narration 'The Romance of Duval Rānā and Khizr Khān'.

The first comprehensive selection of Amīr Khusrau's poetry, *In the Bazaar of Love* covers a wide range of genres and forms, evoking the magic of one of the best-loved poets of the Indian subcontinent.

KAMA SUTRA
A Guide to the Art of Pleasure

Vatsyayana

Translated by A.N.D. Haksar

The ancient guide to the art of living well, in a compelling modern and new translation

Treating pleasure as an art, *Kama Sutra* is a handbook covering every aspect of love and relationships, and was, for centuries, considered an essential part of the well-rounded education of a young, urbane gentleman. Its seven sections are devoted to social life, courtship and marriage, extramarital relations, the conduct of courtesans and prescriptions for enhancing attractiveness, as well as systemic, detailed instruction on sexual techniques.

This new edition of *Kama Sutra* dispels the well-worn image of an erotic Oriental curiosity, highlighting the work's historical importance as a sophisticated guide to living well. Conveying all the original flavour and feel of this elegant, intimate and hugely enjoyable work, this clear, accurate translation is a masterpiece of pithy description and a wry account of human desires and foibles.

Read more in Penguin

I, LALLA
The Poems of Lal Děd

Translated by Ranjit Hoskote

You won't find the Truth
by crossing your legs and holding your breath.
Daydreams won't take you through the gateway of release.
You can stir as much salt as you like in water,
it won't become the sea.

The poems of the fourteenth-century Kashmiri mystic Lal Děd strike us like brief and blinding bursts of light: epiphanic, provocative, they shuttle between the vulnerability of doubt and the assurance of an insight gained through resilience and reflection. The poet Ranjit Hoskote's translation restores the jagged, colloquial power of Lalla's verse, stripping away a century of ornate, Victorian-inflected translations and paraphrases.

I, LALLA
The Poems of Lal Dĕd

Translated by Ranjit Hoskote

You won't find the Truth
by crossing your legs and holding your breath.
Daydreams won't take you through the gateway of release.
You can't hope to reach the self by staying in water.
it won't happen, the sea

The poems of the fourteenth-century Kashmiri mystic Lal Dĕd strike us as brief and blinding as rays of light: epiphanies, provocative, they shuttle between the vulnerability of doubt and the assurance of an insight gained through resilience and reflection. Lal Dĕd, Ranjit Hoskote's translation restores the spare, colloquial power of Lalla's verses, stripping away a century of coyness. Vatsyayan-inspired translations and paraphrases.